Cha Epiphanies
Beyond the horizon of thought

Palak Kothari Shah

BLUEROSE PUBLISHERS
India | U.K.

Copyright © Palak Kothari Shah 2024

All rights reserved by author. No part of this publication may be reproduced, stored in a retrieval system or transmitted in any form or by any means, electronic, mechanical, photocopying, recording or otherwise, without the prior permission of the author. Although every precaution has been taken to verify the accuracy of the information contained herein, the publisher assumes no responsibility for any errors or omissions. No liability is assumed for damages that may result from the use of information contained within.

BlueRose Publishers takes no responsibility for any damages, losses, or liabilities that may arise from the use or misuse of the information, products, or services provided in this publication.

For permissions requests or inquiries regarding this publication, please contact:

BLUEROSE PUBLISHERS
www.BlueRoseONE.com
info@bluerosepublishers.com
+91 8882 898 898
+4407342408967

ISBN: 978-93-6452-204-5

Cover design: Shivani
Typesetting: Sagar

First Edition: September 2024

*This book is dedicated to
my son Arnay and my husband Vishal.*

*Thanks for motivating me, pushing me,
nudging me and sometimes even
threatening me…*

*I swear it would not have been possible
without you guys.*

*I am forever grateful to my lovely family who always
believed in me.*

Love always

Preface

"A poem is like the boat; its meaning like the sea." - Rumi

I believe that poetry has power. It has the ability to convey love, fight hatred, teach lessons or even take you on an imaginary ride. It does not need a plot or so many words like a prose, it can just be brief but filled with ocean full of wisdom. Yet, in spite of being so simple it has creativity immersed in its intricate design. Over the years, learning creative writing and then teaching and mentoring on writing skills to my students, poetry became a universal language and a beloved medium for learning literature.

Ever since my childhood, I had a deep penchant for learning new words. Words evoked a different sense of feeling, seeing them forming into sentences and changing its connotations in different sentences made me even more fascinated. However, poetry gave me solace and a means of expressing my emotions and the love story continues...

Chasing Epiphanies is a collection of some of the poetries that I wrote when I was happy or sometimes when I was lost in reflection or at times when nostalgia took over. These are random musings which got me closer to myself. Added here are also some NaPoWriMo (National Poetry Writing Month) challenges which I thoroughly enjoyed writing. Well, this is my first poetry book and I hope to keep writing further...

All I can say is if it touches a chord with you somewhere then I feel my efforts have reaped its rewards.

The most difficult thing in the world
is being you,
While the easiest thing in the world
Is also being you!

- Palak Kothari Shah -

Contents

Welcome to My World 1

On Writing 2

Doomscrolling 5

Loving, Achieving and Cherishing 6

Every Woman is a Story 9

The Morning I Want to Wake up in 10

The Beach 11

La Soeur (A Sister) 13

My Beautiful House 15

Life is… 17

January 18

Creative Journaling 19

Why Always 20

Neither Hot Nor Cold 21

The Cluttered Brain 23

Those Days 24

Life Is 25

Mistake Worth Forgetting 26

In My Veins 28

I Want to Write 29

Dementia 29

You will be Missed 31

March 32

Good Night 33

Smile	34
That One Time	35
Being Free	36
Travelling Down the Memory Lane	37
She is that Girl	39
I Wish to be a Child Again	42
The Overcast Sky	44
Alone	45
Sometimes	46
Some Days	47
Motherhood	47
Friendship	49
Anniversary	50
Looking Outside	52
What Then	53
I Learnt	54
The Lunchbox	55
The End	57
It Ends with Us, May be?	59
Love on a Different Page	63
The Town Where I Grew up Does Not Exist	67
What I See When I Stare Long Enough into Nothing	71
Love Begins with a Metaphor	73
The Luck of A Chinese Bamboo, A Butterfly and Money	75
Weird Wisdom	79
Wish You Were Here	81
May -December	83

An Ode to My Pyjamas 85

Funny Tourist... 89

Happiness 93

Sadness.. 93

Life 93

Choices 95

White is 99

Black is 100

Destiny Vs Horoscope... 103

Sleeplessness 105

I Wish to be Reborn 109

Dubai... 113

Life is a Poetry... 117

Welcome to My World

With tidbits
of crinkled papers
spread across the floor like
flower petals lying in a park
after the visit of playful winds,
I stare across my inspiration wall,
a plain morning glory paint all over,
where I imagine the thick branches of
lush hot pink bougainvillea with
emerald leaves embracing the wall
from its right corner to the left,
and a sapphire blue door
inviting anyone and everyone
to come without any baggage,
"Enter here and create your world"
it whispers.
Paint it blue or paint it red,
add strokes with your creativity,
outline with your inner feelings,
frame it with your soul,
it is up to you.
You are the artist and you are the canvas.
I am sure,

may be,
one day I will realize
that it was that easy
to create a masterpiece.

On Writing

Writing in, writing out,
a rhythmic dance,
is just how I want
to pass my day

In fact, it is both:
its oh so beautiful strokes
and its deep layered meanings that glow

I often wonder how empty
my life would have been for lack of words
a void of tales, like silent birds,
words give me solace; words give me hope

They tell me every single thing is
just a small part of the big game.
Keep writing! I tell my myself when
nothing goes as per the plan.

I say good times are just here
with every upward stroke,
with every downward stroke I ask myself
to see how pain withers away.

It is as necessary as breathing I say
just as you never stop to
Inhale and exhale.

Writing flows, a stream that bends,
capturing joy and sorrow's plight,
ink the stars, paint the night.
write about the good times and
write about the bad times
write about the best kisses
write about the worst fights
write about the happy songs and the pangs of sorrow.

You exist; therefore, you write...
No wait
I write; therefore, I exist.

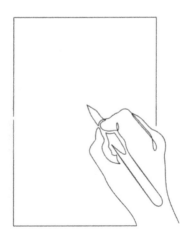

Doomscrolling

I kept scrolling, I kept digging,
The end was nowhere near in this digital jungle.

I kept scrolling, I kept digging,
Hardly aware what I am looking for.

I kept scrolling, I kept digging,
And the time flew without informing.

I kept scrolling, I kept digging,
It now became a habit, an addiction, a way of life

I kept scrolling, I kept digging,
Is there any way to stop? Everything hurts.

I kept scrolling, I kept digging,
There seems no life beyond scrolling and digging.

I kept scrolling, I kept digging,
Everyone went ahead, I am left here!

Loving, Achieving and Cherishing

Dear husband,
It has been a lifetime
we have been always busy.

Busy filling holes
in our mighty sailing ship,
but when one hole is patched
there is another ready to be dealt with.
Let us escape this endless battle
for I don't know if
we are fighting with or against!

We are only getting older
let's have a rendezvous,
a secret one...
and fall in love again.

Let us remain awake a little extra
and look into each other's eyes,
eyes which are now tired
but still filled with love,
with creases of nostalgia
and the puffiness of hope.

Can't we drink coffee
and not speak anything,
just enjoy the bitterness without longing for
sweetness.
Let our silence do the talking
of our struggles and our pains
of our joys and our smiles.

How about we go for that long drive,
where we do not know the destination,
we go as the road goes,
where we stop changing music
and surfing channels,
we let the music speak and the lyrics heal.
Let us soak ourselves in the unknown
after years of only planning.

Let us go to the beaches
and squish our legs in mud
and make an imprint which says
"We were here"
Let the waves wash it over
until we do step again.
We must walk hand in hand
watch the sunsets as if
it's a miracle,
Let us enjoy the little things
after experiencing all those
bigger things.

We are only getting older
Let nothing make us
happy or sad,
let us look back at the
life we created
and show the victory sign!

Every Woman is a Story

Etched upon her face,
every woman bears a tale,
her eyes the only witnesses
sympathize with her soul.
Sacrifices, pains and struggles
easily hide behind her smile,
her scars, an emblem to her valour,
diamonds a tribute to her grace's trial.
Her skin: light or dark
The creases and the lines
emanates the twists and turns of her intriguing plot.
Ageing gracefully, she reaches the climax of her story
finally understands her worth,
gazing for a resolution
to her strong narrative.
But does she ever get a closure of her emotions
or it is always a cliffhanger,
serving as a beginning to someone else's story?

The Morning I Want to Wake up in

Sleepy houses and chirpy birds,
where sky has taken his head out from the blanket
right away,
and the stage is set for the dazzling entry of the sun,
the air so pure, I want to breathe some extra
the grass so lush and dewy, its smells tantalising.
A cup of piping hot tea in hand
with its beautiful aroma dancing on the top,
the first sip of the divine drink
takes all my pains away
just like a rising sun overcomes the darkness.
I want uncreased newspaper with maximum pages
where every turn of page shares
something motivating, something uplifting...
just a few minutes of the day
set for myself- no worries to bother,
that's the morning I want to wake up in.
And when I am done enjoying my company
I want to take a deep breath and say,
"I AM READY"

The Beach

The ultimate union
of the sea and the land,
like a treasure trove of love
it spreads its reach,
trying to cuddle
one and all.

The playfully dancing,
touch-and-go waves
on the mirror-like sea
look cheerful and sparkling,
like a nurturing mother cooing her baby.

Sharing nuggets
one after another,
it teaches fondly,
never saying
the grass is greener on the other side,
preaching contentment and not envy.

It is just perfect;
wherever you are.

It touches the horizon
like a child reaching its mother,
making everything look possible;
within reach.

Unfurling the golden rule of life,
it shares:
the ebb and tide are
the anchors of our being.

Only if you learn to dwell
and embrace without lambast,
wallow in its rhythm
to find the ultimate destination.

La Soeur (A Sister)

There are countless shades of colours,
but a sister is the purest hue of love...

She's not just red, but a scarlet rose,
radiating beauty from her petal thin emotions.

Not merely orange, but a shiny tangerine sun,
emanating brightness with her ever glowing presence.

She's sweeter than yellow, like golden honey,
playful like Bumble bee in our cozy little nest.

She's not just green, but a precious emerald,
a gem so rare and pure.

Not merely blue, but as vast as the expanse of an azure
sky,
her uplifting spirits can dampen all evil.

She's not just indigo but like a peacock's pride,
she walks tall in your every trial.

Not merely violet,
but all the strength of lavender fields.

In this mundane existence
She's a vibrant rainbow of happiness

Together we paint the world with joy and glee,
A sister's love, a masterpiece to feel and heal.

My Beautiful House

A dream that I dreamt always,
To have a beautiful house with majestic hallways.

A house which is state-of-the-art and great,
And so very close to the heart.

A dreamy place where I can be alone.
A cosy place where I can be together and one.

Here I can listen to my own voice
And also, the far and distant noise.

A space which can fit countless memories.
A space which can throw away all negativities.

A destination which you want to reach every day
An abode which you don't want to leave any day

It is made with a lot of hard-earned money
But it surely took a soul to make it a home so sunny

A place that shows me the sunrise and the sunset,
Which teaches me that ups and downs are the pre-set.

When I look down from here, I feel lucky,
When I look up from here, I feel paltry.

Is having your own house a definition of success
Or it is an embodiment of dreams woven into an address.

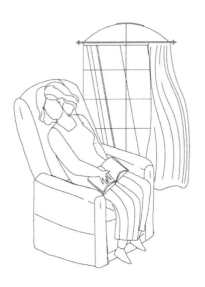

Life is...

Life is like a doodle,
messed up in the beginning
but when you fill the colours
it reveals its beauty and meaning.

Life is like a doodle,
some parts are more colourful
but only when the colourful and dull are together
you can see the magic.

Life is like a doodle,
each part entangled with the other
it shows a million possibilities of one choice
but how the one that you choose is best for you.

Life is like a doodle,
you don't need to think when you do it
let the flow continue its rhythm
to make a beautiful picture in the end...

January

A fresh and clean whiteboard of your life,
ready to be scribbled, decorated and neatly designed.
It knows that its glory will be gone soon
but surely it loves when its celebrated and full blown.
Its anticipation begins a month or more before
knowing its value and virtues and its so many successes stories.
A month unlike any other,
a month of hopes, promises and resolutions.
When asked how it feels like
to be always first in line?
My dear, it says,
just like the first sip of wine.

Creative Journaling

Journaling is a way of life
simplest way to burst your stress bubble
as you put your
heart, mind and soul together
to make your journal spread alive
every page reveals something
passes a message or
just rekindles your conscience
to reiterate what you already know...
It is just magic how
those mossy pages from old tattered books,
unwanted ephemera of memories,
and boring khaki papers
come together to create a
kaleidoscope of emotions on paper.

Why Always

Why does everything happen at its own pace?

Why can't everyday be a deja-vu?

Why can't we know in advance if a heart is going to be broken?

Why is it not possible to know that this will be the last meeting with someone?

Why no one tells us that the one you trust is not a well-wisher?

Why do things unfold like a suspense?

Why do some things happen as a coincidence?

Why can't there be answers for all the Whys?

Why is Why a question?

Why can't Why be an answer...

When it's raining words,
Just shut up
And
Make a story

-Palak Kothari Shah-

Neither Hot Nor Cold

Seasons are only for those
who haven't experienced
the extremes of life,
those who never tasted the dust
nor touched the sky,
for the rest its always
the spring of life
the gift of being alive.

The Cluttered Brain

You can't think right
even when you know
you are wrong,
thousands of thoughts
dart from
all the directions,
each dart carrying with itself
the poison of worries
and arrows of anxiety,
piercing through your brain
making it feel like
the gas chamber of
the nazis.

Those Days

Reliving the olden days
is a bittersweet pill,
it is so easy to laugh at
those painful moments
and
how painful it is
to remember those happy,
cherished memories.
it's true
nothing lasts forever...

Life Is

Life is
but just pain
and
suffering,
The more you endure
the more you live;
pleasure is just a myth.

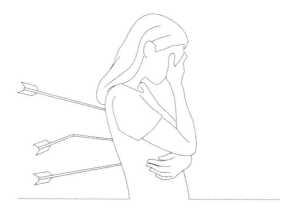

Mistake Worth Forgetting

Sometimes
we choose paths
we know will
lead us to a wrong address,
but we keep going.
In spite of all the
visible red flags
we remain undeterred
as if under a spell.
is it the thrill of that
unchartered territory
or the kindling of
untouched emotions?
We know there will be
a sudden dead end
or an incident
with far reaching consequences
but we keep drifting towards
like addicted souls.
Meanwhile
we keep wishing
for
wrong to become right

but then the bubble bursts
without a boom or a bang
you are bewildered.
Finally,
it ends
you come out
unscathed
unblemished,
you wish to erase it from your
everlasting
memory,
but can you?

In My Veins

Wherever you go
becomes a part of you
somehow...
I wake up in the morning
with the buzz of an alarm,
my eyes closed,
but my hands landing
exactly
on the stop button.
I put my numb
feet on the floor,
to find them exactly
filled in a slip-on.
Just half opened eyes,
in absolute darkness,
I press the switch,
in first attempt,
and open the bathroom door!
this is my home
where I moved a month back
and now
it runs in my veins.

I Want to Write

I want to swim deep
into the oceans of thoughts,
dive into the innermost caves
and find the rarest oyster.
I want to fight hard
against the pirates of distraction.
I want to survive
the tsunami of ambiguity.
I want to kick from the depths
and soar with confidence.
I want to stay away
from the iceberg of impostor.
I want to come to the shore of writing victorious.

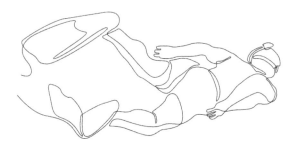

Dementia

Blank eyes
staring into nothing.
Once trusted
memory betrays,
how can one understand
the pain of not knowing the known,
the sufferer, a bag of bones,
gazes the horizon
oblivious to the end.

You will be Missed

You will be missed,
always and forever.

You will be missed
when the evening breeze
swirls through my hairs and neck
just like your magical touch.

You will be missed
every time I see a smile
which emanates from eyes
and sparkles with childlike innocence.

You will be missed
when I need that extra cheering,
those unwanted pushes and nudge,
and sweet taunts filled with love.

You will be missed
when I am alone or in crowd
in darkness or in light
wherever there is love.

March

It comes with a warm ray of hope

Once frozen, the flowers now show signs of life

Come evening and the breeze brings a pleasant aroma

A stroke of colour fills the otherwise grey canvas

The humble sky welcomes the change with shades of rose, lavender and cerulean

The land is now ready to burn itself

To make a passage for rains

Finally, its summer time!

Good Night

Yesterday,
in my dream
I met myself.
I asked her, "What are you doing?"
She said, "Nothing, worrying about worries"
I said, "Let us go to sleep, worries will fly away"
But we gave each other company
and the sleep flew away.

Smile

Your smile
is a
seed
which
sprouts
leaves of hope
in my heart.

That One Time

You might be that person with a golden heart,
But that one time...

You might be the one who rescues everyone from trouble,
But that one time...

You might be the one who ticks all the right boxes,
But that one time...

You might be the one who can brighten up lives,
But that one time...

And for this one time,
I can't forgive you.
I can't trust you.
I can't love you.

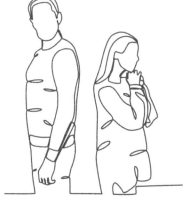

Being Free

Being free is not just
absence of a cage.
Sometimes there are
dangerous
invisible barriers,
which others may not see!
They might feel that you
act on your will,
but in reality
you are a puppet
moving on the behest
of what others want.
Never underestimate
or fail to cherish
when you experience
even
an iota of freedom!

Travelling Down the Memory Lane

Imagine revisiting the city
you grew up in...
The school where you once studied,
has stood the test of time.
Even with its freshly painted walls
the old stories,
still intact.
Everything has changed
but it is still the same.
The college from which you graduated
has some new feathers in its cap,
but it still remembers you
and is privy to your secrets.
Just like all those places
significant part of your growing up
the places where you binged your
most soul satisfying meal
or the unselfish shade of that humble tree
underneath which you could
open your heart with your friends,
a part of me still resides

here and a part of my heart beats for this place
Even after so many
time lapses
it is steadfast to its roots.
then there were those places we never liked
but now love begins on a fresh slate
I feel the pleasure of visiting
an old place
far exceeds that of meeting old friends
because
places don't hide anything
and the
unsaid remains unsaid.

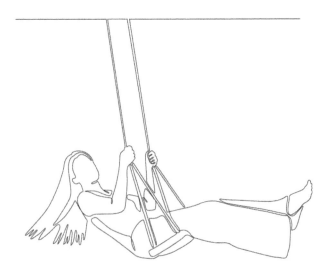

Life is like a rear-view mirror
You can glance at past
But can't remain fixated
You need to look
A-H-E-A-D

- Palak Kothari Shah -

She is that Girl

She is that girl,
Oh yes!
With her you can experience
love at first sight,
She is the one
who won't say "yes" easily...
But once she giver her heart,
She will shed tears with you and sing along your
happy tunes.
She will hide her pains when you're happy
She will sacrifice with a smile
and will laugh with a jerky tear
She will begin with you
and end with you
A melange of dream and reality
Too good to be true
Your alter ego
She is that girl...
But
She is that closed book
Waiting to be opened

To be read and enjoyed
To be understood and grasped
To be nurtured and cared for
To be the love and to be loved...

I Wish to be a Child Again

How I wish
to be a child again
to see the world
with wonder and awe...
to bring the innocence back,
to love without expectations,
and forget hate in a jiffy,
Being carefree again;
to unlearn how to worry.
Play till my heart's content,
and live as if there is no tomorrow.
I want to trust sans doubts,
believe that the world is a beautiful place...
I want to flash smiles and tears
whenever I want
I want to speak out my mind
without any fears...

Why do we change when we grow up?
Where does the endless energy and zeal go?
How did we end up under the
heaps of worries and stress...
Innocence got replaced by shrewdness,
friendships emerged from calculations,

love became weakness,
Why do we forget that
we are here for a limited time,
we are here to rise together.

The Overcast Sky

Every writer's muse
is an overcast sky
where the clouds bow down
to kiss the earth.
A sudden chill in the atmosphere
sends birds into a frenzy,
wondering if it is time already.

Lightning strikes
as an alarm for war,
thunder roars
as a harbinger of doom.
The world transforms into
a slice of dark fantasy;
it feels as if a dragon is
just ready to show up!

The first few drops of rain escape,
making way for the floods of thought.
the sky pours to its heart's content,
until it has drenched itself of all emotions.

Alone

When no one is there
and you are alone,
actually,
you are not alone
but your deepest feelings are with you.
You believed that
they are long lost,
buried in the quagmires of reality...
They are still there,
Safely tucked in the deepest corner
of your heart
They come and greet you
When you are alone!

Sometimes..

Sometimes,
I want to go back in time
and
rectify, mend, repair
things, emotions, broken hearts

Sometimes,
I want to run far away
from everything
so far
that there is no trace of me

Sometimes
I want to peep into the future
and want to assure myself
not to fall
into overthinking

Sometimes,
I just want to be myself
forgetting what others will
think, say and do.

Some Days

Some days
you feel like
a piece of paper
amidst strong winds
going everywhere
and settling nowhere

And on some other days
you feel like
a flower
nodding in the gentle breeze
of the spring
spreading its fragrance.

Live any ways.

Motherhood

They say,
it takes a village to
raise a child...
But I feel
It takes
A million sacrifices
Tons of crushed ambitions
And daggers of pain
to raise a genius!

Friendship

Friendship
makes life a mosaic out of
those incomplete jigsaw pieces,
It brings home
a symphony of music
from the unspoken words
and hidden wishes,
It conquers everything
in its path to
gain supremacy
in your heart.
In fact,
friendship is like an art.
No form
No material
No rules
Just pure connection.

Anniversary

Today, while we were on our morning walk
You asked me,
"So how did your past twelve years with me go?"
I reply
"Well, they went exactly like our morning walk"
We began our journey with hopes, dreams and joys...
Alas!
Every journey can't be just
full of beauty and love,
there is always some unwanted
dirt and garbage on the way...
And yes!
sometimes there can be
detours; or may be
We had to start everything from scratch
But no detour can deter us...

You know the best part
With you is when we wander aimlessly,
When we are not afraid to try
Nor are we pressed for time...
That's when you are at your best-fully present.
The road had its own curves and twists

There were potholes and bumps
There were narrow lanes and broad horizon
There were barking dogs who seldom bite
To always keep us cautious.
We run together and we walk together
We sigh together and we giggle together
If we are together
Then any journey is surmountable
In the end, it's just the sight of our goal
Our home
That keeps us going

Looking Outside

I look outside of my glass window
sitting in my safe haven,
its scorching heat outside;
But I feel untouched by the cruelty.
The canvas of the sky is clear
changing colours to only mark the time
I see how buildings outline the sky
slowly trying to conquer the supremacy...
So many people like me
would be staring from their windows,
but no one would be thinking like me,
because we are not only different from outside
but also, on the inside.

What Then

We all love to motivate and
Inspire people,
People buried in depression
People with low self-worth
People who have lost all hope...
We like to be their guiding light.
But what then
When they bypass everyone's expectations
And rise higher,
Even above you...
Would you still be happier?

I Learnt

I learnt to rise,
Even after I felt bogged down from the burden.
I learnt to keep my eyes wide open,
Even when they begged for some repose.
I learnt to cook meals for hungry mouths,
Even when my stomach was barren.
I learnt to dust away my pains,
Even after I had the worst falls of life.
I learnt to show a brave face,
Even when I was scared to death.
I learnt to flash my smile,
Even when I was down in the dumps.
I learnt to be rightful,
Even when I could choose the easy path.
I learnt to feel pretty,
Even when I felt the least.
Truly, in motherhood lies profound lessons!
For there is someone
Who loves me
unconditionally
in spite of everything.

The Lunchbox

The lunchbox
is a metaphor of love
from a bride to her husband
filled with ambrosia of emotions
in the warmth of homecooked food.
A parcel which once
opened
starts sharing the aromatic stories
of desire, longing and love,
the way the feelings are packed in the
the crumples of *rotis*
revealing in one-pleat after another,
with sweet nothings and naughty banters
melting in the luscious *aloo-matar*,
reminding of the first kiss
in the first rains
the husband can see how the coy bride
must have added
the flavour to the rice from the
tempering of that extra roasted *jeera*
while the tangy dal of happiness is ready
to mingle,
and as if the love was brimming out

and irresistible,
heavenly morsels of dessert
whisper
I miss you in its every bite.

The End

The end is
time-honoured like a sundown
inevitable as the last page of a book
unknown as the depth of an ocean
perpetual like the wheel of a bicycle
neither virtuous nor corrupt
it is the sincerity of truth
conclusiveness of the apt closure,
It is something
we had always wanted,
waited for,
asked for,
desired for.
But
it arrives only
after the heights of crescendo
are conquered,
imparting the wisdom of discipline
or recompensating with bounty
end is justice
delivered,
Moral of the universe.

NaPoWriMo Challenge

Challenge: _Without consulting the book – write a poem that recounts the plot, or some portion of the plot, of a novel that you remember having liked but that you haven't read in a long time._

It Ends with Us, May be?

Random picks, sometimes,
can lead to instant clicks.
One fine day
came into my way
the story of a not so meek
female protagonist never afraid to speak,
Lily Bloom was her name
and she had her dad to blame...
No! not just for her silly name
but for his cunning game.
Abuse and victimisation she grew up with
deciding to never accept the myth,
until she meets Ryle
and forgets her every trial.
Neck deep in love and affection
all her nightmares seemed to go for correction,
a beautiful owner of a beautiful business
she was best in her finesse,
until her past comes back
and the present takes aback.
She finds herself in her mother's plight
unfazed between wrong and right,
will she rise up or accept things as fate

her dilemma written in words that weigh
but Lily decides to break the bloom
rising above to not accept the doom,
she decided to not be her mother
when she herself becomes a mother!
Ending the cycle of abuse
she healed her bruise.
Dear Colleen Hoover,
I agree IT ENDS WITH US,
could have been better with
IT ENDS WHEN YOU END IT...

NaPoWriMo Challenge

Challenge: *Write a platonic love poem. In other words, a poem not about a romantic partner, but some other kind of love – your love for your sister, or a friend, or even your love for a really good Chicago deep dish pizza. The poem should be written directly to the object of your affections (like a letter is written to "you"), and should describe at least three memories of you engaging with that person/thing.*

Love on a Different Page

Dear Journal
Without you my life would be empty as a Vanity Fair,
Showy but insignificant!

Like the first rains of monsoon
you decided to oblige my dull being
and my life bloomed
as fragrance of petrichor,
spreading across my mind and my soul.

How I come to you
like a blank canvas
and return back as a deep thought masterpiece
gaining sanity and wisdom
with each mindful spread.

I snuggle you with me
wherever I go
I still remember the first time we met
I was like a scaredy neophyte
clueless, scratching my head.
You held your arms open
letting me in with my inhibitions.

I know I owe you a big time
as the other day
when I was in need of comfort and solace
you came as a cascading waterfall
of words, rhyme and art
so peaceful and so healing

Sometimes I drown you in mix of random colours,
the other time I stick those ephemeras,
at times it could be an aimless doodle

Journey with you is a meaningful mystery
and destination- an exciting beginning...

NaPoWriMo Challenge

Challenge: *The Town Where I Grew up Does Not Exist*

The Town Where I Grew up Does Not Exist

In fiery summer heat,
on my two-wheeler,
masked in a cotton white *dupatta,*
over my face and my head
I scurried through the
Known and unknown streets of my town;
I was drenched in the sweat of enjoyment and
wallowed in the warmth of joy.

But today as I slide
in an air-conditioned car
through the concrete jungle
that has worn the mask of a mega city
I feel lost...

Everything has got a makeover.
Everything has lost its soul.
Those narrow jovial lanes
are now stretched to its limits.
The prosperous green boulevard
now a shadow to tall metallic blocs,
that big old banyan tree

left for heavenly abode before its time.
Gazing in my eyes with puzzled emotions
I feel like my city is asking me,
"Do we know each other?"

NaPoWriMo Challenge

Challenge: What I See When I Stare Long Enough into Nothing

What I See When I Stare Long Enough into Nothing

All I want to do in this life
is to stand and stare,
stare into those prairies
which is endless in itself,
stare till the sky changes colours
till I can see nothing,
because that's when i see everything
beyond and beneath.

NaPoWriMo Challenge

Challenge: Love Begins with a Metaphor

Love Begins with a Metaphor

Love at first sight
Butterflies in the stomach
Starry eyes
Intimate love
To the moon and back
Takes my breath away
It is true, love begins with a metaphor
And slowly
It reverberates with
Reality
Compromise
Ego
Understanding
Heartache
Insecurity
Letting go
And transpires into paradox.

NaPoWriMo Challenge

Try your hand at writing your own poem about how a pair or trio very different things would perceive of a blessing or, alternatively, how these very different things would think of something else (luck, grief, happiness, etc).

The Luck of A Chinese Bamboo, A Butterfly and Money

Its luck and nothing else
says the Chinese bamboo,
that I become humongous
in a short span.
So, what if no one sees that
I grow inside first before
I grow outside.

Its luck and nothing else
says the butterfly,
that I am one of the most
beautiful creations of nature.
So, what if no one sees that
I was once just an
ugly, fat and hungry insect.

Its luck and nothing else
says money
That everyone thinks about me
day and night

So, what if they don't know
that I never go to anyone
without them paying a price.

NaPoWriMo Challenge

Challenge: you to write a poem rooted in "weird wisdom," by which we mean something objectively odd that someone told you once, and that has stuck with you ever since.

Weird Wisdom

Childhood days
with carefree laughter
I did not have
For inside my mouth
Was a big giant tunnel
As big as a truck could pass.

I smiled when others laughed
I giggled with hands on my mouth
And it became a habit!

Till I met someone
Who made me laugh endlessly
He said I am in love..
With the beautiful gap
Between your teeth
I stopped laughing...
Don't you know, my dear
He said,
It is lucky
To have a gap
between those front teeth!
And I never stopped laughing...

NaPoWriMo Challenge

Challenge: *Write a poem titled "Wish You Were Here" that takes its inspiration from the idea of a postcard. Consistent with the abbreviated format of a postcard, your poem should be short, and should play with the idea of travel, distance, or sightseeing.*

Wish You Were Here

Even the boons
and blessings
of technology
cannot save a relationship,
entangled
in the web of distance;
if people lose
hope...
Wish you were here,
witnessing those distant stars
we always saw together.
Today I am alone,
and the stars are closer than you.

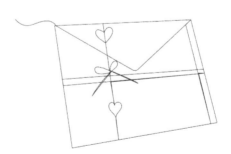

NaPoWriMo Challenge

Challenge: Today, we challenge you to write a poem that centers around an encounter or relationship between two people (or things) that shouldn't really have ever met — whether due to time, space, age, the differences in their nature, or for any other reason.

May -December

You are May,
I am December.
We are like vehicles on the road
coming from different directions.
which meet for fleeting seconds
and go in their own journey,
We can never be together.

Our chance meeting
was a chance
when we both decided to rest half way
But now neither can I
nor can you
wait any further.

Let us become strangers
Again
till our death
and let us meet
Again
to unite souls
Again.

NaPoWriMo Challenge

Challenge: *Write your own ode celebrating an everyday object.*

An Ode to My Pyjamas

Touch so soft as woven with finest water,
feel as docile as touch of a feather,
I feel you are made with memory,
as every time I wear You
You remember the curves
and roadblocks to the T
You fit
just
as one would like it.
One happy fitting outfit you are!

Your chequered look
with uniform print
all over
makes me feel seamless and one...
You never envied fashion;
Simplicity your friend,
I know what makes you feel sad
A broken button in the middle.
But whoever said was right
That pyjamas are the
most compassionate and tolerant being
Sometimes you give me company

till the noon,
when I am lazy and feel so dull.
Sometimes I wear you early
when it is raining
and no one is to come
and nowhere is to go
You, me, books and coffee
with a soft, sepia lamp
We make a shining troupe.

NaPoWriMo Challenge

Challenge: Write a poem based on one of the curious headlines, cartoons, and other journalistic tidbits featured at <u>Yesterday's Print</u>, where old new stays amusing, curious, and sometimes downright confusing.

The tourist is funny. He tries to "do" a foreign city in 24 hours, though he has learned little about his own city in 24 years.

Funny Tourist

Everybody, Everywhere
wants a piece of this planet...
Everyone wants
to be a tourist and
to click grammable pictures.
And to convey and imprint,
"I was here".
Tourists are crazy.
Tourists are everywhere.
Must-visits,
Bucket lists,
Fear Of missing out...
How can you explore a place in 24 hours
while it took centuries for it to be what it is today.
Why are you always in a hurry,
spend some time,
look at their sun rises and sun sets
get into the skin of the place.
Don't just see but feel the aura.
Don't just smell but inhale their culture.
Don't just hear but listen to their stories.
Don't just touch but feel its elements.
Don't just taste but imbibe their flavours.

That's when you can claim,
Yes, I know this place.
Otherwise it is just like us
How we know about space and planets,
But do we know what is inside us!
We are also the star we need to know...

NaPoWriMo Challenge

Challenge: Write a monostich, which is a one-line poem, or a poem made up of one-liner style jokes/sentiments. Need inspiration?

Happiness

The Anticipation of happiness brings happiness.

Sadness

When that happiness goes to someone else, it brings sadness.

Life

Happiness or sadness, live your life as it is just one short eternity.

NaPoWriMo Challenge

Challenge: Write a poem that begins with a line from another poem (not necessarily the first one), but then goes elsewhere with it.

Choices

I took the road less travelled by,
and that took me to places
I never thought of.
'It is all about the choices'
the path echoed.
The journey was gruelling,
the untrodden walkway
had its own share of pebbles and boulders.
With Insurmountable peaks
And bottomless troughs
there were deafening noises
which disheartened the will
there were warnings
that predicted downfall
there was unfavourable weather
to make things worse
but when I learnt to ignore
and let the sunshine enter through the foliage
all the doubts vanished
and the obstacles faded into mirage
leading the way to
a life
rich with contentment and harmony

'You must live the choices you make,'
Endorsed life.
For on those roads less taken
Lies the treasure unfound.

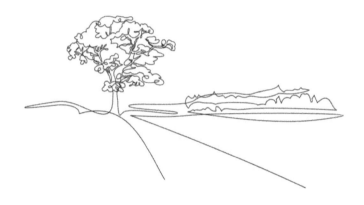

NaPoWriMo Challenge

Challenge: Write a poem that repeats or focuses on a single colour.

White is

White is the epitome of love in the pristine marbles of the Taj Mahal

White blankets the sleepy town in a glowy-snowy hug

White is the tickly and soft foam in a sleek bath tub that delights instantly

White is the fluttering clean bedsheet hanging on a clothesline dancing on the happy song

White is the embellishment of the smooth and bumpy *chikankari* embroidery which elevates any attire

White is the luminosity of freshly whitewashed wall enlightening everything nearby

White is the picturesque desert of salt which touches the horizon with its crystalised dreams

White is the crisp page of a new unwritten journal ready for the new beginnings and old endings

White is the wiseness in hairs of my grandma and her so many enigmatic stories

White feels like a shade and shield of an umbrella in scorching heat

White tastes like the mild and mellow soft vanilla which melts instantly

White are the refreshing flowers decorated on a prayer plate ready to be offered to the lord
White is the feeling of purity and peace and piousness
White is endless and ethereal
White makes me feel forever optimistic...

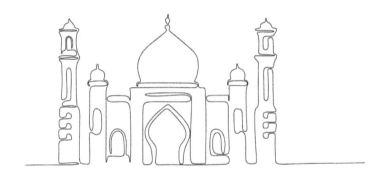

Black is

Black is the long moon less night waiting for the dawn
Black is the kohl adorning the eyes of a damsel
Black is the luscious long hair that love to go on adventures
Black is the endless ink which fills the oceans of diaries
Black is the soothing koel chirping for its beloved
Black is the velvety touch of a bear's fur
Black is the smell of brewed coffee and its everlasting taste
Black is the darkness and infinity of the universe
Black is the skin colour of gods own creations
Black exists so that others can shine

NaPoWriMo Challenge

Challenge: *The idea is to write a poem in which two things have a fight. Two very unlikely things, if you can manage it. Like, maybe a comb and a spatula. Or a daffodil and a bag of potato chips. Or perhaps your two things could be linked somehow – like a rock and a hard place – and be utterly sick of being so joined. The possibilities are endless!*

Destiny Vs Horoscope

Horoscope said,

"Come to me and unveil your future."

Destiny argues,

"No need to go, we design our own future."

Horoscope convinces,

"I can predict if there is any unforeseen hurdle."

Destiny retorts,

"Hurdle is hurdle only if you think of it as hurdle"

Horoscope pleads,

"There is nothing wrong in being prepared for the storm."

Destiny yields,

"The true fun lies in embracing the unknown."

Horoscope insists,

"Into the stars lies your path to glory!"

Destiny concludes,

"Dreams are a born from the passion within..."

Napowrimo Challenge

Challenge: *What are you haunted by, or what haunts you? Write a poem responding to this question. Then change the word haunt to hunt.*

Sleeplessness

It is dark
pitch charcoal ink black all around
A gleam of hope emanates
Will sleep be my guest today!

The thought provokes
a train of unending engines of reflections.
It takes me on a time travel spree
when I am a shy introverted child
Who is lonely;
And does not know if she is sad or happy
The other times it's the waterfall of youth
that flows out of my every cell
oozing confidence of a bright bright
future...
While unknowingly comes those times
I never lived but I wished I could.
May be if I was in a different tangent of life,
Sleeplessness just haunts me...

The idea that today also I might remain awake
Tossing and turning like a fish which
got washed out on the shore and

longing to hit the waves again,
To regain its drained energy
And fill the body with dreams

Closing my eyes tight like
the cork in a bottle of wine
also does not help in intoxication;
not even those forty winks come to visit.
Night passes quickly;
No sleep, no wink

The weird wisdom of ages
counting backwards
and catching breath
catches me in a whimsy.

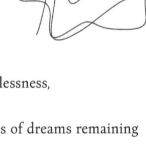

I want to sleep
and hunt down my sleeplessness,
cut it down to pieces
where there are no shards of dreams remaining
It is just dark,
pitch charcoal ink black all around.

NaPoWriMo Challenge

Challenge: Write a poem in which the speaker expresses the desire to be someone or something else, and explains why.

I Wish to be Reborn

I wish to be reborn
as a bright and tall
Sunflower...
To live in full bloom
wherever life plants me.
Simply,
following the light
from morning to night
enduring the test of time.
Always soothing, always healing,
lifting spirits high...
Wrapped in wisdom and warmth.
I wish
to be the epitome of happiness
with my luck and charm.

As infinite as the endless horizon.
A flower without thorns, unfaded.
A promise to be there.
Inspiring artists and poets alike
with eternal beauty..
I wish to be reborn
as a Sunflower

to be
radiant in crowds
and
hopeful in solitude.

Napowrimo Challenge

Challenge: *Write a poem in which you closely describe an object or place, and then end with a much more abstract line that doesn't seemingly have anything to do with that object or place, but which, of course, really does.*

Dubai

Here I come to you,
Oh! Land of mystical magic.
You created an oasis from
the parched, plain lands,
your progress a testimony,
that even stone yields water.
Skyscrapers adorn your skyline
And luxury flows on roads,
like a Midas touch, everything
you touch turns into gold...
You created oceans and forest in
a dry and acrid land.
People all over the world throng here
Or have put you in their bucket list.
I look forward to making lifetime memories
in different corners of
your world-
in a lightning universe
or the humongous delicate skyscrapers,
In the lanes of old bazar
to the throbbing gigantic malls,
those mindboggling adventure parks
and that heart melting desert safaris

I wish to leave
A part of my heart
in those unknown lanes of perfection.

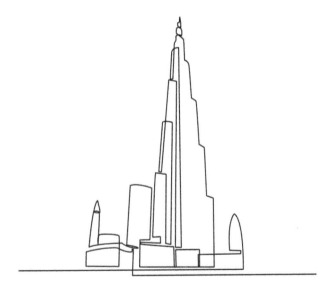

NaPoWriMo Challenge

Today, we'd like to encourage you to take a look at *@StampsBot*, and become inspired by the wide, wonderful, and sometimes wacky world of postage stamps.

Life is a Poetry

Life is a poetry-
sing along
match your tunes!
Life is a poetry-
keep rhyming
those happy moments
Life is a poetry-
make your own jingles
as you hum along your tales.
Life is a poetry-
Rejoice!
cause you never know when it ends...

So beautiful is the journey that

I would not like to reach the destination

- Palak Kothari Shah -

Milton Keynes UK
Ingram Content Group UK Ltd.
UKHW031120261124
451585UK00004B/355